TEXAS LONGHORNS

BY J CHRIS ROSELIUS

Printed in the United States of America,
North Mankato, Minnesota
052012
092012

THIS BOOK CONTAINS AT LEAST 10% RECYCLED MATERIALS.

Editor: Alex Monnig
Series Designer: Craig Hinton

Photo Credits: Jamie Schwaberow/AP Images, cover, 7, 9, 11, 43 (bottom right); AP Images, 1, 18, 20, 23, 24, 28, 43 (top left), 43 (top right); Kiichiro Sato/AP Images, 4; Aaron M. Sprecher/AP Images, 12; BES/AP Images, 15; Carl E. Linde/AP Images, 17, 42 (top); Rich Clarkson/Sports Illustrated/Getty Images, 26, 42 (bottom); Eric Gay/AP Images, 31; George Bridges/AP Images, 33, 43 (bottom left); Harry Cabluck/AP Images, 34, 39; Denis Poroy/AP Images, 37; Amy Gutierrez/AP Images, 41; Mario Cantu/Cal Sport Media/AP Images, 44

Library of Congress Cataloging-in-Publication Data
Roselius, J Chris.
Texas Longhorns / by J Chris Roselius.
p. cm. -- (Inside college football)
ISBN 978-1-61783-504-9
1. University of Texas at Austin--Football--History--Juvenile literature. 2. Texas Longhorns (Football team)--History--Juvenile literature. I. Title.
GV958.U5862R67 2013
796.332'630976431--dc23
2012001857

TABLE OF CONTENTS

Texas wide receiver Limas Sweed, *left*, makes a fourth-quarter touchdown catch in the Longhorns' 2005 win over Ohio State.

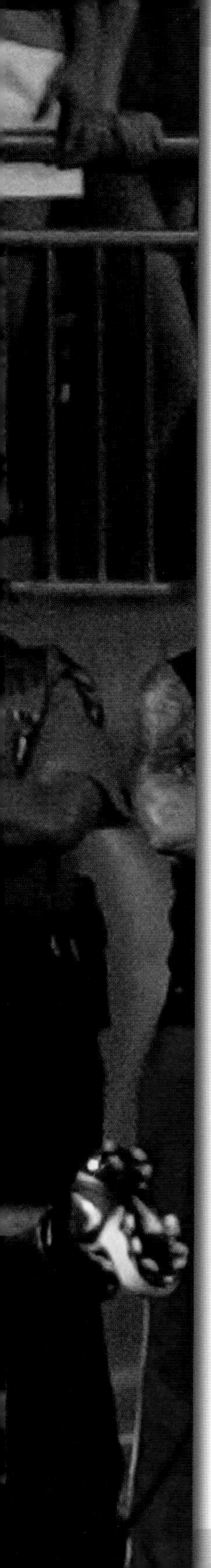

1

TEXAS-SIZED COMEBACK

THE TEXAS LONGHORNS HAVE BEEN ONE OF THE TOP TEAMS IN COLLEGE FOOTBALL SINCE THEIR FIRST GAME IN 1893. HEADING INTO THE 2005 SEASON, THE PROGRAM HAD 787 WINS. THAT PLACED IT NEAR THE TOP OF THE ALL-TIME WINS LIST IN NATIONAL COLLEGIATE ATHLETIC ASSOCIATION (NCAA) DIVISION 1-A FOOTBALL. WINNING WAS EXPECTED AT TEXAS.

But in 2005, the Longhorns were not expected to just win. They were expected to contend for the national title. Entering the season, Texas was ranked second in the Associated Press (AP) Poll. The AP Poll and the Coaches' Poll are considered the most respected polls in college football. The Longhorns wasted little time proving they deserved that ranking. They defeated Louisiana-Lafayette 60–3 in the season opener.

The win set up a showdown against fourth-ranked Ohio State in Columbus, Ohio. Texas junior quarterback Vince Young was the star. He threw two touchdown passes, including a 24-yard pass to sophomore receiver Limas Sweed with 2:37 remaining in the fourth quarter. Texas left Columbus with a 25–22 victory. And that would be the fewest points the Longhorns would score all season.

Texas followed that win with easy victories against Rice and Missouri. The Longhorns then demolished rival Oklahoma 45–12 before defeating Colorado, Texas Tech, Oklahoma State, Baylor, Kansas, and Texas A&M. All of those victories meant Texas got to again play Colorado in the Big 12 Conference Championship Game.

The Longhorns dominated from start to finish. Young threw for three touchdowns and rushed for one as Texas rolled past Colorado 70–3. That earned Texas a berth in the Bowl Championship Series (BCS) title game. The BCS is a computer system used to match up the best teams at the end of the season. That year, the two best teams in the BCS would meet in the Rose Bowl.

Young and the Longhorns had been in the spotlight all season. Over in the Pac-10 Conference, the University of Southern California (USC) Trojans were the other marquee team that year. Fans had been waiting

AN AMAZING COMEBACK

On October 29, 2005, the Longhorns watched Oklahoma State build a 28–9 lead in the first half. But quarterback Vince Young sparked an amazing comeback with an 80-yard run in the third quarter. Texas scored the game's final 38 points to win 47–28. Young ended the night with a career-high 267 rushing yards. He also threw for 239 yards.

Texas quarterback Vince Young eludes USC tacklers during the 2006 Rose Bowl.

for months to see Texas and USC play each other. Now, the two teams would finally meet—with the national championship on the line.

USC had won back-to-back national titles in the two years prior. They were in the midst of a 34-game winning streak. Many people believed the Trojans were one of the best teams of all time. They featured a backfield of senior quarterback Matt Leinart and junior running backs Reggie Bush and LenDale White. Leinart won the Heisman Trophy in 2004 as the nation's top college player. And Bush was the Heisman winner in 2005.

But the Trojans did not have Young.

He proved to be the difference in the game. Young, who finished second to Bush in the voting for the 2005 Heisman Trophy, was a dynamic player. He had amazing speed, and he eluded tacklers when he ran. He also threw the ball well. He did all of those things against USC.

"Vince Young is a great football player and, to me, the most valuable player on our team, and on any team in the country," Texas coach Mack Brown said after Texas won the Big 12 title. "I don't think we would be sitting here today without Vince."

The Longhorns trailed USC 38–33 with 26 seconds left in the game. Young stood five yards behind center waiting for the snap. The Longhorns needed to convert on fourth-and-five from the Trojans' 8-yard line. A perfect 13–0 season and the national title were on the line.

Taking the snap, Young looked into the end zone for an open receiver. But many of the 93,986 fans watching the game in the Rose Bowl did not expect Young to throw. And they were right.

Young saw an opening around the right side. He pulled down the ball and eluded one USC defender behind the line of scrimmage. He then outran another defender into the right corner of the end zone for a touchdown.

"We kept our poise," said Texas junior right tackle Justin Blalock, "put the ball in Vince's hands, and let the man do what he does."

Young's touchdown run was an exclamation point on an outstanding night. He finished the game with 267 passing yards and completed 30 of his 40 passing attempts. He also rushed for 200 yards on 19 carries.

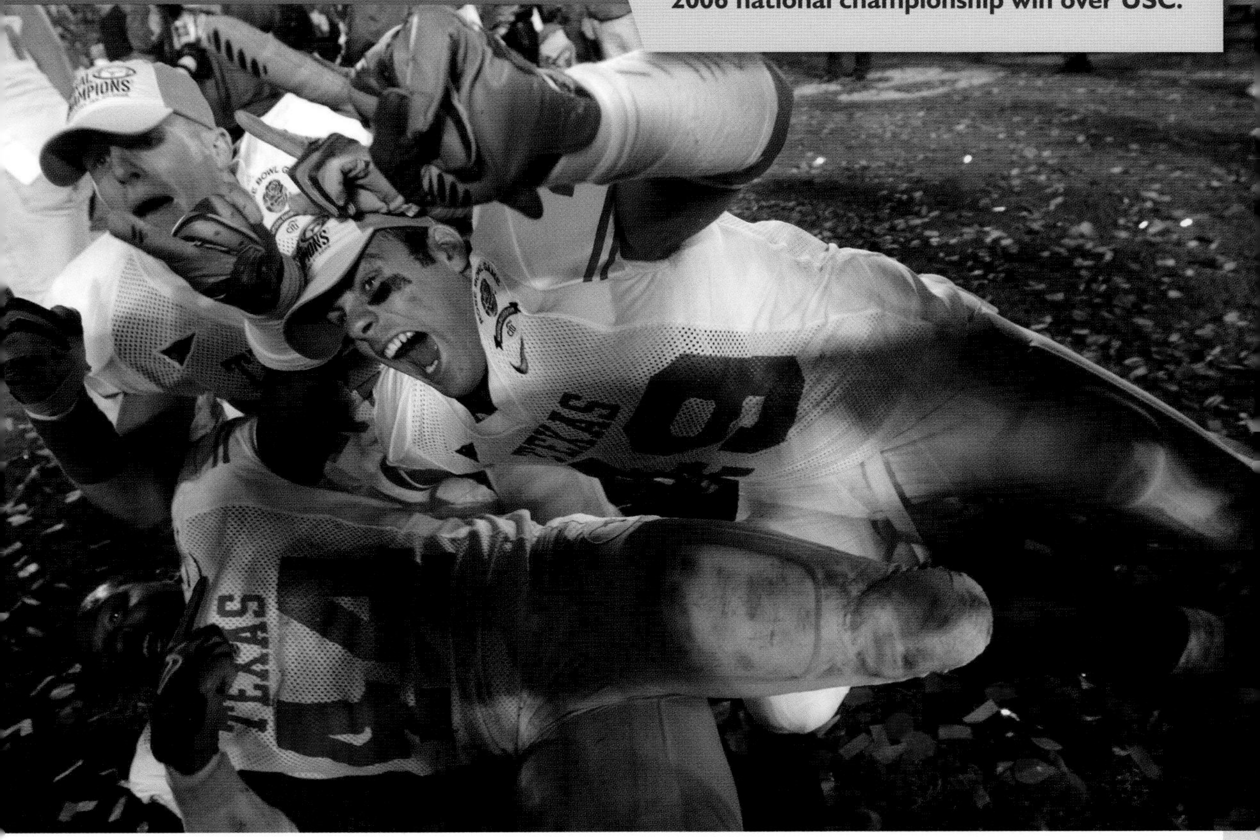

Rashad Bobino, *bottom*, Eric Hall, *right*, and Braden Johnson, *left*, celebrate Texas' 2006 national championship win over USC.

Young scored on a two-point conversion to stretch the lead to 41–38 with 19 seconds left. Texas would hold on to win its first national title since 1970.

Young's last-minute scamper into the end zone capped a fantastic comeback by the Longhorns. The Texas defense had trouble stopping the Trojans all night. Because of that, Texas trailed 38–26 with 6:42 remaining in the game. But Young led the Longhorns down the field and scored on a 17-yard run. The extra point pulled the Horns to within five with 4:03 remaining.

WHAT A CAREER

During his three-year career at Texas, Vince Young did just about everything a player could do. He led the Longhorns to a perfect 13–0 record in 2005 to win the national title. He won the Maxwell Award as the nation's top player. He won the Davey O'Brien Award as the nation's top quarterback. But he fell just short of winning the Heisman Trophy, finishing second to Reggie Bush of USC in 2005.

Young repeatedly came through in the clutch for Texas. During his career he led the team to eight wins when the team was tied or trailing at halftime. One of those comebacks came against Kansas. The Longhorns trailed 23–20 with just over a minute left in the game. On fourth-and-18, Young scrambled out of the pocket and ran for 22 yards and the first down. Four plays later he threw a 21-yard touchdown pass to win the game.

It still looked like the Trojans were going to win, though. USC got the ball to the Texas 45-yard line with 2:13 left in the game. It was fourth down. All USC needed was two yards to keep the drive going and run out the clock. The Trojans had scored on all four of their possessions in the second half. So USC coach Pete Carroll decided to go for the first down instead of punting.

Leinart took the snap and handed the ball to White, who tried to run up the middle. The Longhorns sent every defender toward the line of scrimmage. There they ran into White and stopped him short of the first down. The Texas defense had finally stopped USC.

Texas took control of the ball with a little more than two minutes remaining. Young then guided the Longhorns down the field for the winning touchdown.

"I can't imagine leaving Texas in a better way," senior defensive back Michael Huff said.

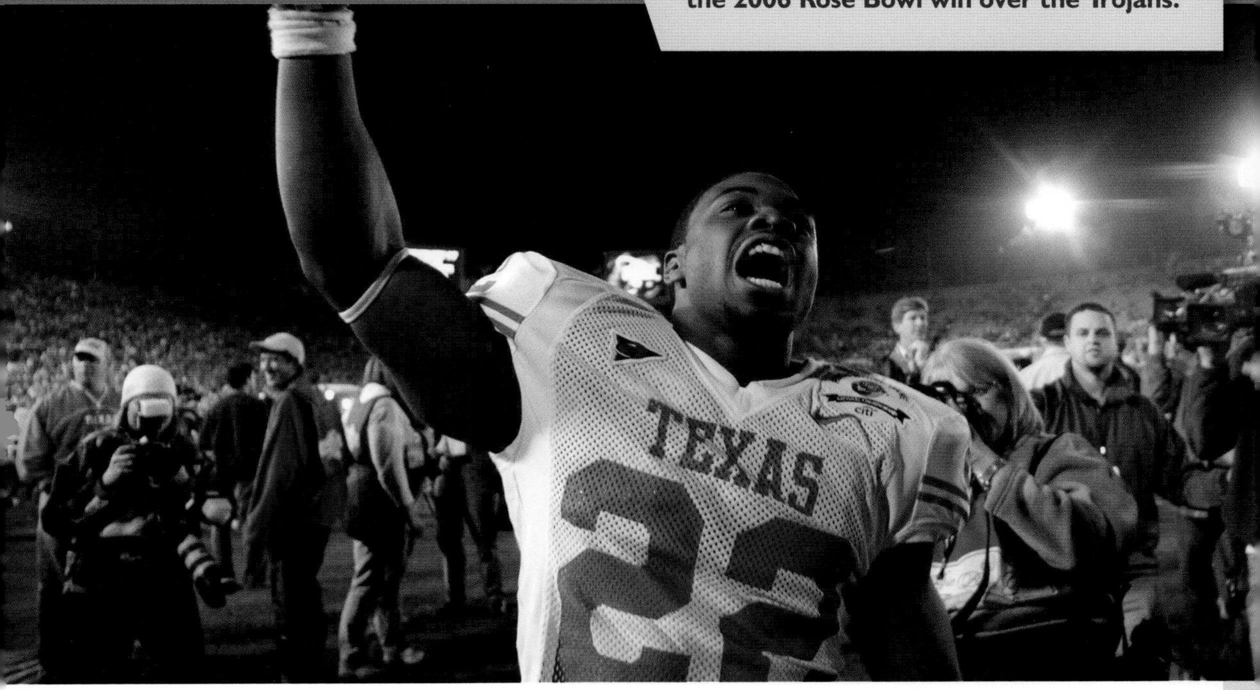

Longhorns running back Selvin Young rushed for 45 yards and a touchdown in the 2006 Rose Bowl win over the Trojans.

Young was voted the Most Valuable Player (MVP) of the game, but he was not the only star for the Longhorns against USC. Junior running back Selvin Young and sophomore running back Ramonce Taylor combined for 57 rushing yards and two touchdowns. Senior tight end David Thomas caught 10 passes for 88 yards. And Sweed added eight receptions for 65 yards.

The game would be the final one for Young as a Longhorn. He decided to head to the National Football League (NFL) a few weeks later. But Texas fans will always remember what he did against USC in the Rose Bowl on January 4, 2006.

Texas played football for ten years before becoming known as the Longhorns.

2

THE BEGINNINGS OF A POWERHOUSE

ON NOVEMBER 30, 1893—THANKSGIVING DAY—THE UNIVERSITY OF TEXAS PLAYED ITS FIRST FOOTBALL GAME. THE TEAM WAS KNOWN AS "THE VARSITY." THEY TRAVELED FROM THEIR HOME IN AUSTIN, TEXAS, TO DALLAS, TEXAS, TO FACE THE DALLAS FOOTBALL CLUB. DALLAS WAS EXPECTED TO WIN. BUT TEXAS SURPRISED EVERYONE BY WINNING 18–16. APPROXIMATELY 2,000 FANS WATCHED THE GAME.

The win started a tradition of success at Texas. Inspired by the victory over Dallas, the team quickly scheduled three more games for the season. Texas defeated a team from San Antonio, Texas, twice and then again faced Dallas. Texas once again prevailed, this time 16–0.

Texas played rival Texas A&M for the first time on October 19, 1894. Texas cruised to a 38–0 victory. Those two teams would go on to become fierce rivals, playing every year from 1915 to 2011, when Texas A&M left the Big 12 Conference.

STORY OF THE LONGHORN

When Texas first started playing football in 1893, the team was called "the Varsity." It was a nickname that lasted for 10 years. In 1904, a sportswriter for the *Daily Texan*, the school newspaper, used the nickname "Longhorns" when he referred to the football team. The use of the nickname stuck, but it was not until 1916 when the longhorn steer became the university's official mascot.

Texas lost only one game in its first three seasons. In fact, the Longhorns did not suffer a losing season until 1933. From 1893 to 1910, Texas won 102 games while losing only 31 and tying seven.

While Texas won year after year, it was rare for a coach to last more than two or three seasons. That is, until Dave Allerdice took over in 1911. He compiled a 33–7 record in five seasons as coach.

Allerdice left after the 1915 season because he did not like the pressure of coaching the Longhorns. Texas then went through two coaches before Berry Whitaker took over in 1920. He established Texas as a football power. In his first season, Texas finished 9–0 overall and 5–0 in Southwest Conference (SWC) play to win the conference title. Texas was nearly as successful the next two seasons. The Longhorns went 6–1–1 in 1921 and 7–2 in 1922. But Whitaker decided to step down after the 1922 season. He claimed the stress of coaching was too much to handle.

The winning continued under coaches E. J. Stewart and Clyde Littlefield. In four seasons as coach, Stewart guided Texas to a 24–9–3

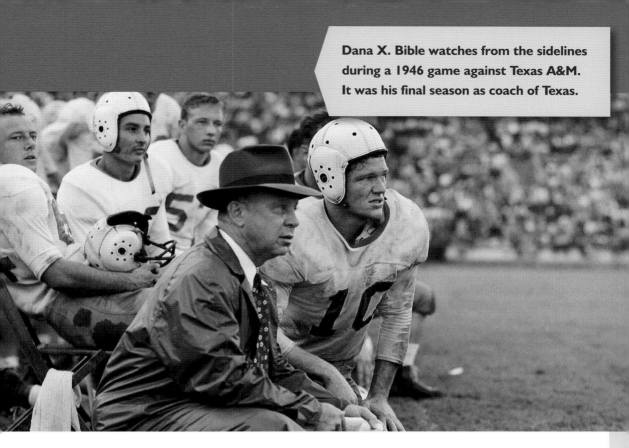

Dana X. Bible watches from the sidelines during a 1946 game against Texas A&M. It was his final season as coach of Texas.

record. Littlefield then took over in 1927. During his seven years as coach, Texas won two SWC titles and went 44–18–16. But in 1937, Texas again needed a new coach. It found the perfect one in Dana X. Bible. He had previously led Texas A&M and Nebraska to a combined 11 conference titles.

Texas won only three games during Bible's first two years as coach. But the team improved to 5–4 in 1939. A 14–13 victory over powerful Arkansas was a turning point for the program. With the game nearly over, sophomore running back Jack Crain caught a short pass and raced 67 yards for a touchdown. Texas then added the extra point for the win.

In 1941, the Longhorns reached the number-one ranking in the AP Poll. That was the first time the team had ever been the top-ranked team in the country. Texas finished ranked fourth in the final AP Poll with an 8–1–1 record. The 1945 team was the first squad to win 10 games.

Bible decided to retire after the 1946 season. He finished his career at Texas with a 63–31–3 record and three conference titles. He also went 2–0–1 in three Cotton Bowl appearances. In 1941, the Cotton Bowl started featuring the winner of the SWC each year. In 1943, Bible took Texas to its first of many Cotton Bowls. It was also the school's first ever bowl game appearance.

Blair Cherry, a member of Bible's coaching staff since 1937, took over as coach. Bobby Layne, the senior All-American quarterback, led the Longhorns to a 10–1 record in 1947. They beat sixth-ranked Alabama 27–7 in the Sugar Bowl. The Sugar Bowl is one of the most prestigious bowl games. The Longhorns finished the year ranked fifth.

Texas finished 7–3–1 the following season and defeated number eight Georgia in the Orange Bowl. The Orange Bowl is also an important bowl game. In 1950, the Longhorns went 9–2 overall and a perfect 6–0 in conference play to win the title.

THE IMPOSSIBLE CATCH

On November 28, 1940, the Longhorns faced Texas A&M in their traditional Thanksgiving showdown. On the third play of the game, Texas junior back Noble Doss hauled in an over-the-shoulder pass reception—a play known as the "impossible catch." Junior fullback Pete Layden then scored on a 1-yard run as Texas defeated A&M 7–0. That broke the Aggies' 19-game winning streak.

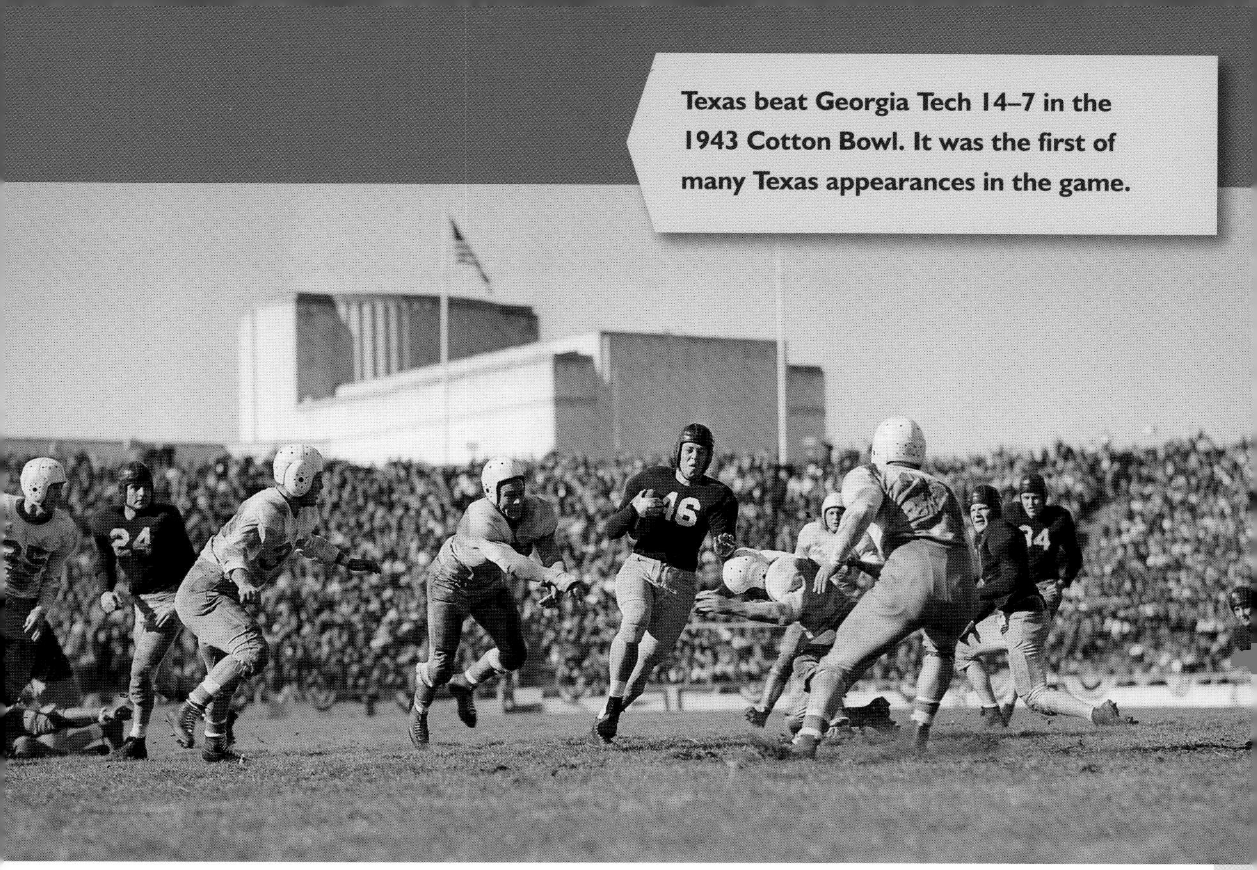

Texas beat Georgia Tech 14–7 in the 1943 Cotton Bowl. It was the first of many Texas appearances in the game.

They finished the year ranked third in the AP Poll and second in the United Press International (UPI) Poll. The season ended with a loss to fourth-ranked Tennessee in the Cotton Bowl. It was Cherry's last game. He retired to enter the oil business. Cherry ended his career with a 32–10–1 record.

Ed Price took over the program in 1951 and picked up where Cherry left off. In his first three seasons, the Longhorns won two conference titles and the 1953 Cotton Bowl. But the Longhorns were just a combined 10–19–1 in his final three years. Price resigned after the 1956 season. The Longhorns replaced him with Darrell Royal. A glorious era in Texas football was about to begin.

As a sophomore, linebacker Tommy Nobis helped Texas win its first national championship in 1963.

3

AN ERA OF CHAMPIONS

THE HISTORY OF TEXAS WAS CHANGED FOREVER IN DECEMBER, 1956, WHEN THE TEAM HIRED DARRELL ROYAL TO BE ITS NEW COACH. AT AGE 32, ROYAL WAS ONE OF THE YOUNGEST COACHES IN COLLEGE FOOTBALL. BUT HE TURNED THE LONGHORNS INTO A NATIONAL POWER.

In his first season, Royal led the team to a 6–4–1 record, a berth in the Sugar Bowl, and a final ranking of eleventh in the AP Poll. Running back James Saxton was Royal's first standout player. Saxton finished third in the Heisman Trophy voting in 1961 as a senior. That year, he led the team to a 10–1 record and a number-three ranking.

The Longhorns finished the season ranked outside the top 20 in the AP Poll just six times during Royal's 20 years in Austin. They finished ranked fifth or better seven times from 1961 to 1970. But what separated Royal from previous Texas coaches was the fact that he won national titles. The Longhorns won three championships with him.

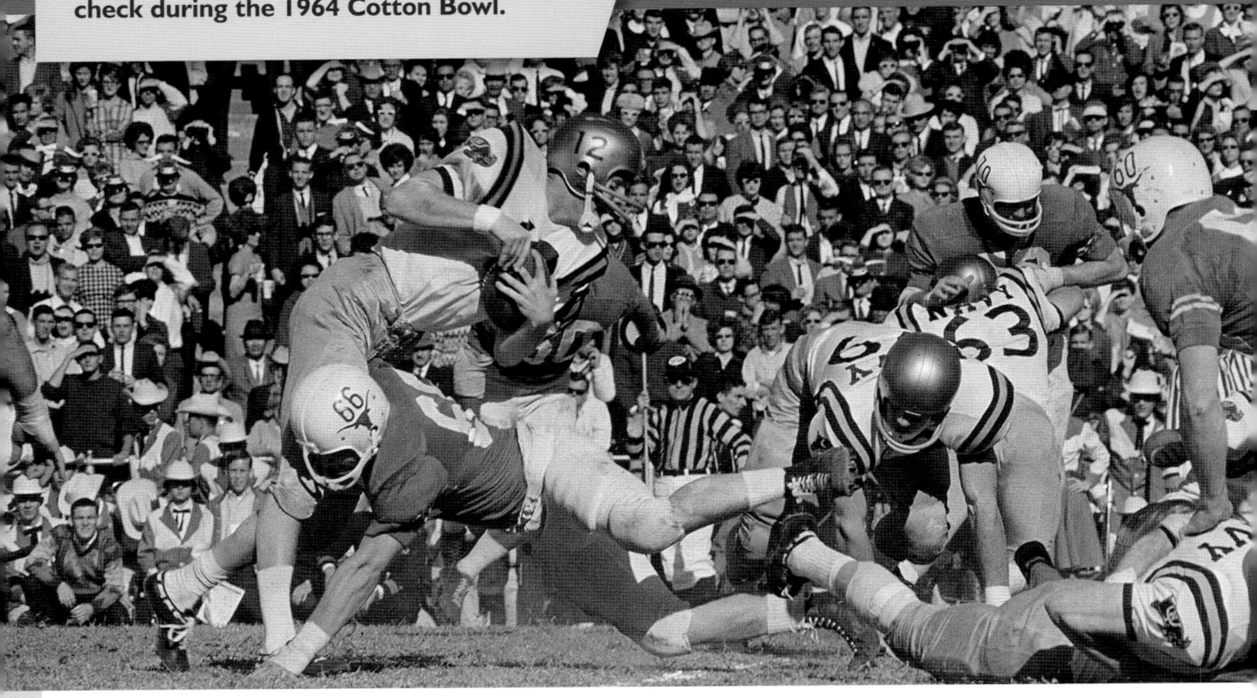

Texas held Navy's Heisman Trophy-winning quarterback Roger Staubach in check during the 1964 Cotton Bowl.

Thanks in large part to the play of sophomore linebacker/guard Tommy Nobis, Texas won its first national title in 1963. Nobis is considered by many to be the best Longhorns linebacker ever. He was named All-American twice and was a three-time All-SWC player. Nobis was the leader of a team that went 11–0. The defense allowed just 71 points all season. No team scored more than 13 points in a game against Texas that year.

But the road to the title was not easy. Texas was ranked second after starting the season with three impressive wins. The team rose to number one after beating the top-ranked Oklahoma Sooners 28–7. It was a ranking the Longhorns would not lose. Texas finished the regular season undefeated. Unlike today, the AP and UPI Polls were final at the end of the regular season. That meant the Longhorns were national champions before their Cotton Bowl matchup with number-two Navy. That team was led by junior Heisman Trophy-winning quarterback Roger Staubach.

Most expected the game to be close. But the Longhorns dominated from start to finish. Senior tackle Scott Appleton and Nobis forced Staubach to scramble all game. And on offense, senior quarterback Duke Carlisle threw for 213 yards and two touchdowns in the 28–6 victory.

"I've never seen a team which deserved to be number one more than Texas," Navy coach Wayne Hardin said after the game. "Texas was just the best we've played, that's all. Staubach didn't play as well as usual, but I imagine Texas had a lot to do with that."

Despite losing Nobis, Carlisle, and Appleton, Texas finished 10–1 in 1964. The top-ranked Alabama Crimson Tide were named the national champions that year. But Texas got a chance to face them in the Orange Bowl.

1,000 X 3

Running back Chris Gilbert (1966 to 1968) became the first player in NCAA history to rush for at least 1,000 yards in three consecutive seasons. He might have had four straight seasons of 1,000 yards, but freshmen were not eligible to play back then. A three-time team MVP, Gilbert finished his career as Texas' and the SWC's all-time leading rusher with 3,231 yards.

IN MEMORY OF FREDDIE STEINMARK

Safety Freddie Steinmark started for the Longhorns as a sophomore and junior in 1968 and 1969. A key contributor to the team, Steinmark was diagnosed with bone cancer one week after helping Texas defeat Arkansas to win the 1969 national title.

To combat the cancer, his left leg was amputated at the hip. Less than one month later, Steinmark, with the help of crutches, stood on the Texas sideline to cheer the team to victory over Notre Dame. Coach Darrell Royal presented Steinmark the game ball.

Steinmark battled cancer for the next year and half before dying in June 1971. In his memory, every Longhorn player touches a picture of him placed on the scoreboard as they head to the football field before each home game.

Senior quarterback Joe Namath led undefeated Alabama. But like Staubach one year earlier, Namath struggled against Texas. The Longhorns built a 21–7 halftime lead. They held on for a 21–17 victory.

The Longhorns went 9–1–1 in 1968. Royal installed a new offense called the wishbone to take advantage of the running skills of senior back Chris Gilbert and junior quarterback James Street. The offense featured a fullback and two halfbacks. The quarterback could hand the ball off to the fullback, one of the halfbacks, or keep the ball himself.

Texas started the season 0–1–1 while getting used to the new offense. But a 31–3 win over Oklahoma State started a streak of 30 consecutive victories and back-to-back national titles in 1969 and 1970.

Texas finished the 1968 season with nine straight wins. The Longhorns started the 1969 season ranked fourth.

President Richard Nixon gives a plaque to Texas coach Darrell Royal after Texas won the 1969 national championship.

They took over the top spot in the AP Poll after a 69–7 win over Texas Christian University on November 15. After a 37-point victory over Texas A&M on Thanksgiving Day, the Longhorns faced second-ranked Arkansas on the road.

Texas had won 18 games in a row. Arkansas had won 15 straight games. President Richard Nixon attended the matchup to award the national title to the winning team. The Longhorns trailed 14–8 midway through the fourth quarter, and they faced a fourth–and–three from their own 43-yard line. Street threw a 44-yard pass to senior tight end Randy Peschel for a first down. Two plays later, sophomore back Jim Bertelsen scored on a two-yard run. Junior Happy Feller added the extra point to give the Longhorns a 15–14 lead they would not give up.

Texas coach Darrell Royal wanted to use Texas' running backs more, so Emory Bellard invented the wishbone offense.

Texas capped its second national title of the decade and its five-hundredth win as a program with a 21–17 win over number nine Notre Dame in the Cotton Bowl.

Then, the team claimed its third national championship and second straight UPI title in 1970 by finishing the regular season 10–0. The Longhorns outscored foes 412–125 that season. But starting that year the final AP Poll would not be conducted until after the bowl games.

Texas had to beat number six Notre Dame in the Cotton Bowl to finish first in the AP Poll. Unlike the previous season, the Longhorns failed to slow down the Fighting Irish. Notre Dame snapped Texas'

30-game winning streak with a 24–11 victory. Texas, which finished first in the UPI Poll, shared the national championship with Nebraska, who finished first in the AP Poll.

The Longhorns won three more SWC titles from 1971–73. They ran their streak of consecutive Cotton Bowl appearances to six. But Texas struggled in 1974. The team failed to win the conference title for the first time since 1967. The Longhorns bounced back to finish 10–2 and win a share of the SWC title in 1975. But they dropped to 5–5–1 in 1976.

Royal retired after that season. He never suffered a losing season in his 20 years at Texas. The Longhorns went 167–47–5 during his tenure and were 109–27–2 in SWC games. Texas won three national titles, 11 conference titles, and appeared in 16 bowl games under Royal. Fans now expected national championships. Those high expectations made life tough for the next three Texas coaches.

GAME-CHANGING OFFENSE

After the 1967 season, coach Darrell Royal asked assistant Emory Bellard to come up with an offense that would have a lead blocker and take advantage of the team's talented runners. Bellard came up with what is today called the wishbone offense. It features the quarterback and three running backs in the backfield who line up in a "Y," or "wishbone," formation.

Unveiling the new offense in 1968, Texas tied its first game and then lost its second. The Longhorns then won 30 straight games and back-to-back titles thanks to the wishbone. Several of the best team rushing seasons in Texas history came between 1968 and 1975, when the Longhorns featured the formation.

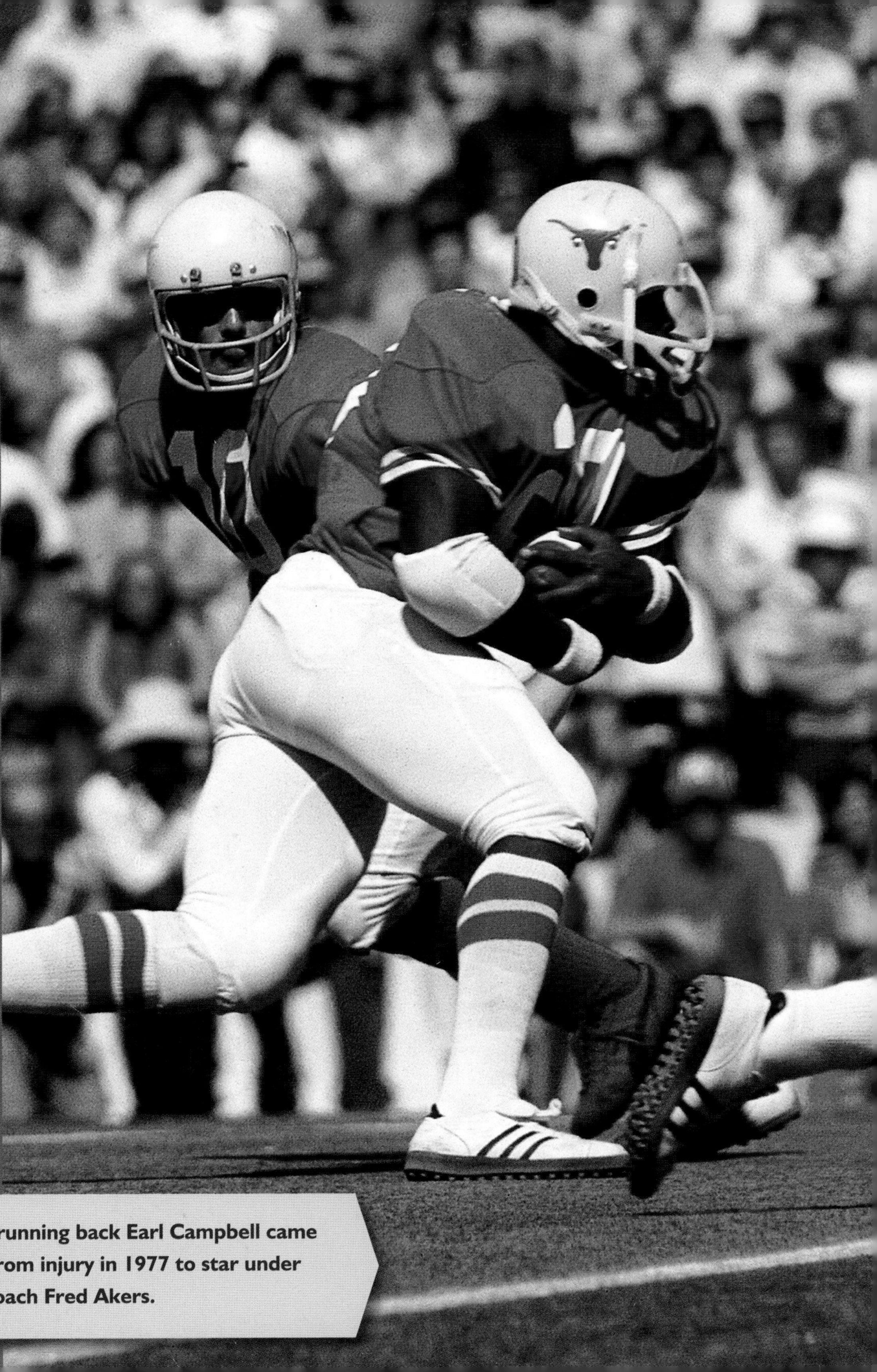

Texas running back Earl Campbell came back from injury in 1977 to star under new coach Fred Akers.

4

FALLING SHORT AGAIN, AND AGAIN

THE RETIREMENT OF DARRELL ROYAL LEFT A VOID IN THE TEXAS PROGRAM. TEXAS DECIDED WYOMING'S COACH, FRED AKERS, WOULD FILL IT. HE HAD SPENT TIME AS AN ASSISTANT COACH ON ROYAL'S STAFF.

Akers quickly showed he would do things his way when he took over in 1977. He switched his offense to the "I" formation to take advantage of the talents of senior running back Earl Campbell.

Campbell had two productive seasons under Royal. As a freshman in 1974, Campbell started at fullback in the wishbone offense and rushed for 928 yards and six touchdowns. As a sophomore, he rushed for 1,118 yards and 13 touchdowns and earned All-America honors. Injuries derailed Campbell's 1976 season.

But he was fully healthy in 1977 and produced an amazing season in Akers's first season as coach. Campbell led the

In 1977, Fred Akers, *left*, was named Coach of the Year and Earl Campbell, *right*, won the Heisman Trophy.

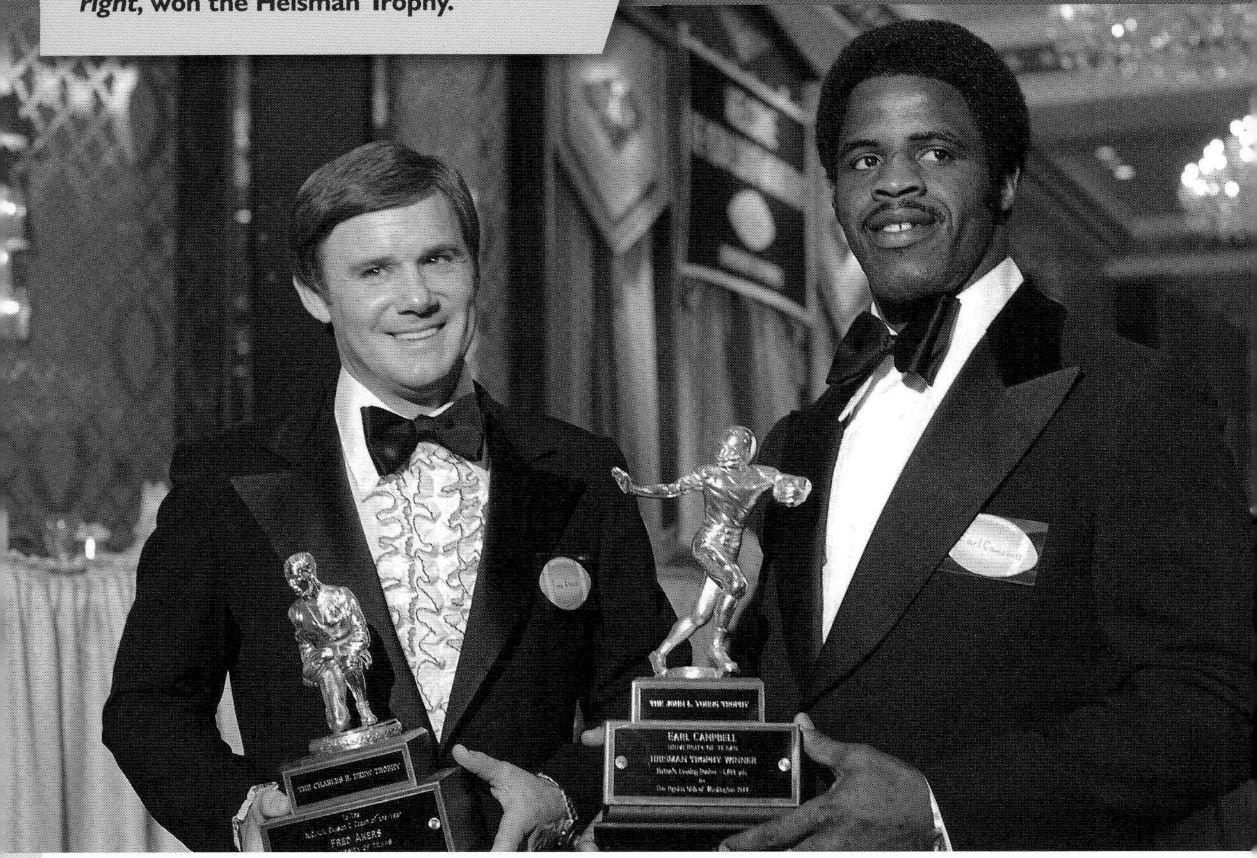

Longhorns to within one game of the school's fourth national title. He led the nation in rushing with 1,744 yards. That year he topped 100 yards rushing 10 times. He also became the first Texas player to win the Heisman Trophy.

Thanks to Campbell and a strong defense, the Longhorns outscored their first three opponents 184–15 to move up to fifth in the AP Poll. Texas then defeated number two Oklahoma 13–6 in their annual matchup. Campbell rushed for 124 yards and scored the team's lone touchdown on a 24-yard run.

Another outstanding game from Campbell came against Texas A&M that year. He rushed for 222 yards and four touchdowns. He even added a 60-yard touchdown reception on a screen pass—the only touchdown reception of his career.

The Longhorns finished the regular season undefeated and ranked number one in both the AP and UPI polls. Texas had to beat fifth-ranked Notre Dame in the Cotton Bowl to win the national title. But Texas lost 38–10. Campbell rushed for 116 yards on 29 carries but did not score. The Notre Dame defense had three interceptions and shut down the Texas offense.

The 11–1 finish was the first of nine straight winning seasons and bowl game appearances under Akers. A strong defense lifted the 1981 Longhorns to a 10–1–1 record. They defeated third-ranked Alabama in the Cotton Bowl. The Longhorns ended the year ranked second in the AP Poll and fourth in the

"THE TYLER ROSE"

Texas great Earl Campbell grew up in Tyler, Texas. He was the fifth of 11 children raised by his mother, Ann. Tyler is known as the "City of Roses" and is home to the Municipal Rose Garden. Nearly 40,000 rose bushes bloom from late April until the first frost of the season. In fact, more than 100,000 people from around the world visit the Rose Garden in Tyler each year.

Because Campbell called Tyler home, he was given the nickname "The Tyler Rose." He even wore a Rose on his lapel while becoming the first Texas player to accept the Heisman Trophy in New York City in 1977. Campbell led the nation in rushing that year with 1,744 yards. He ended his college career with 4,443 yards. On November 24, 1979, Texas retired his No. 20 jersey at the Longhorns' game against Baylor.

UPI Poll. After going 9–3 in 1982, Texas finished the 1983 regular season a perfect 11–0. The defense was outstanding once again and was led by senior tackle Tony Degrate.

That year the Longhorns faced number seven Georgia in the Cotton Bowl. Second-ranked Texas held a 9–3 lead late in the fourth quarter. But Georgia recovered a fumbled punt at the Texas 23-yard line. The Bulldogs scored with 3:22 remaining to win 10–9. Top-ranked Nebraska also lost that day. The Longhorns would have won the national championship if they had beaten Georgia.

Texas suffered key injuries in 1986 and finished just 5–6. Akers was fired after that season, despite owning a record of 86–31–2 and twice coming within one win of the national championship.

The team then turned to another former Longhorn to take control. David McWilliams was hired away from Texas Tech. He had been one of the captains on the 1963 national title team. He had also been an assistant coach for both Royal and Akers.

DID YOU KNOW?

Peter Gardere is the only Texas quarterback to beat arch-rival Oklahoma four times. He guided the Longhorns to a come-from-behind win in 1989 as Texas beat the Sooners for the first time since 1983. Gardere rallied the Longhorns to victory again in 1990 in a 14–13 win. Texas then beat the Sooners 10–7 in 1991 and 34–24 in 1992. In his final game against the Sooners, Gardere threw for 274 yards and two touchdowns.

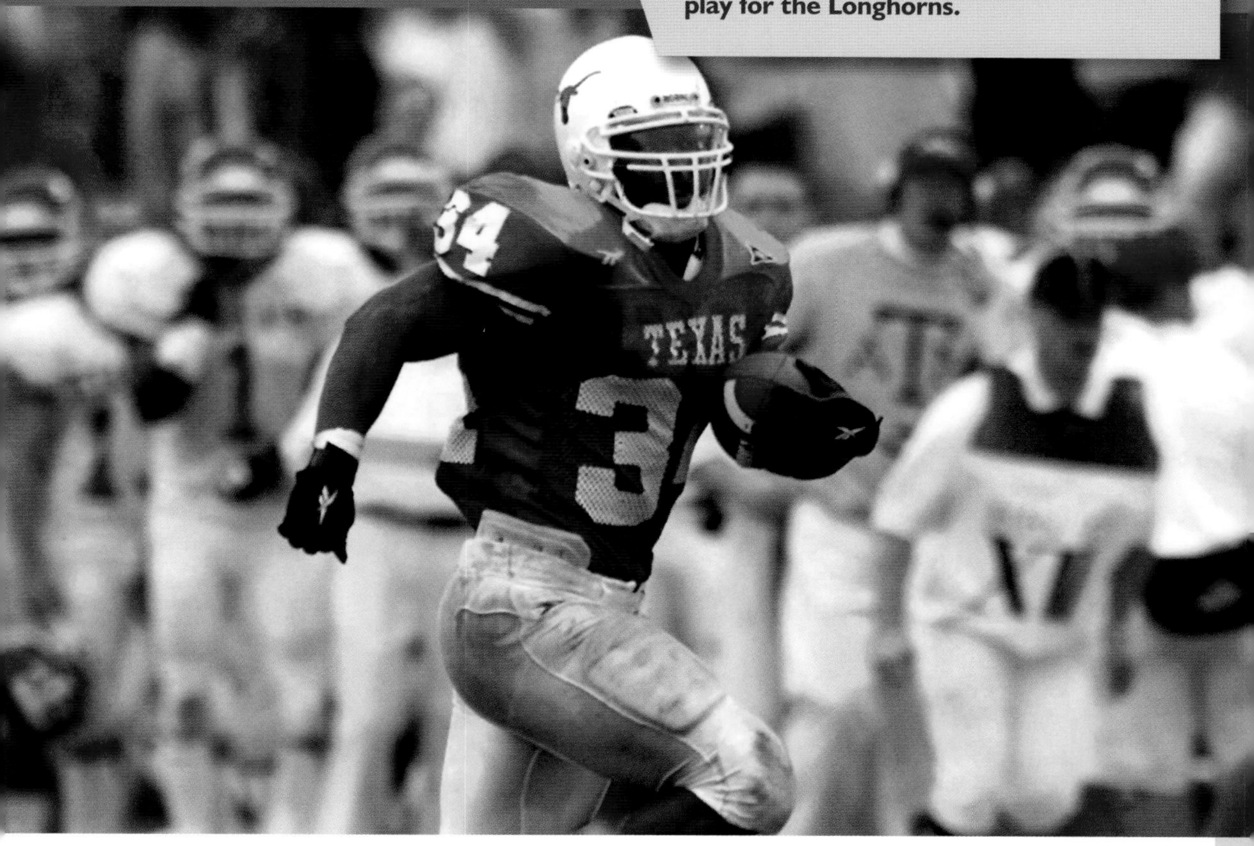

Texas coach John Mackovic helped convince running back Ricky Williams to play for the Longhorns.

McWilliams produced one winning season during his first three years. But in 1990, led by sophomore quarterback Peter Gardere, the Longhorns finished 10–1 and won the SWC title. The turning point in the season was a 14–13 win over number four Oklahoma.

The Longhorns closed out the regular season with nine straight wins. But third-ranked Texas was blown out 46–3 by fourth-ranked Miami in the Cotton Bowl.

The Longhorns fell to 5–6 the following season and fired McWilliams. He finished his five years at Texas with a 31–26 record.

Unlike Akers and McWilliams, new coach John Mackovic had no previous ties to the Longhorns. But while at Texas, he recruited some of the best offensive players the program has ever known. Players such as running back Ricky Williams, quarterback James Brown, and receiver Mike Adams played under Mackovic.

Mackovic's best seasons came in 1995 and 1996. The Longhorns went 10–2–1 in 1995 and won the final SWC title. The conference broke apart after the season. Texas and former SWC teams Texas A&M, Texas Tech, and Baylor merged with the teams in the Big Eight to form the new Big 12 Conference. The eighth-ranked Longhorns entered the season as one of the favorites to represent the South Division in the first Big 12 Conference Championship Game.

Texas did not live up to expectations early. The team started the season 3–4 overall and 2–2 in conference play. But behind the passing of Brown and a running game that featured sophomore Williams and senior Priest Holmes, the Longhorns won four straight games to win the Big 12 South Division title.

The Longhorns faced number three Nebraska in the conference championship game. The two-time defending national champions were huge favorites. But the Longhorns won 37–27. Brown threw for 353 yards, and Holmes rushed for 120 yards and three touchdowns.

The key play in the game came with 2:48 remaining in the fourth quarter. The Longhorns faced fourth-and-inches at their own 28. Mackovic decided to go for the first down. Instead of running the ball,

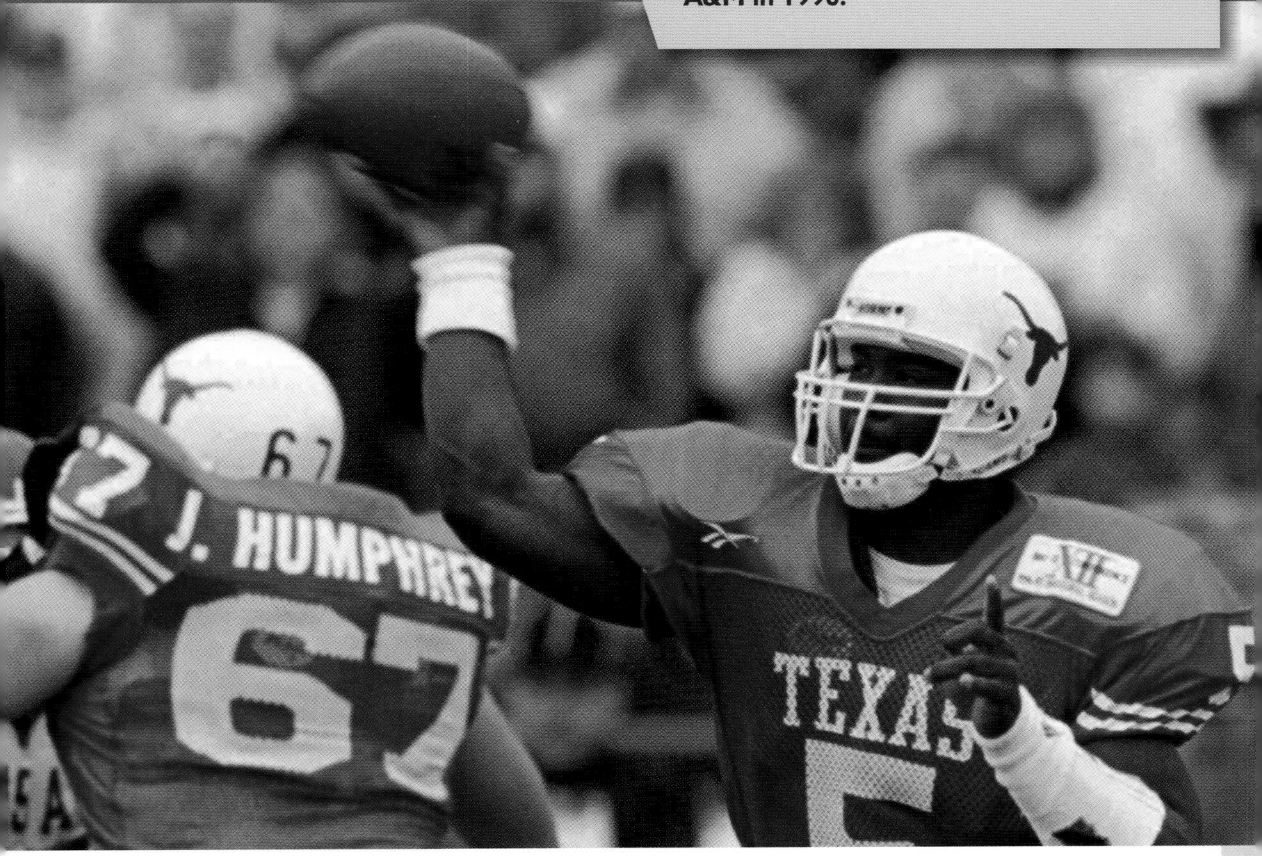

Texas quarterback James Brown throws a pass in the team's 51–15 win over Texas A&M in 1996.

Brown rolled to his left and found a wide-open Derek Lewis. He hauled in the short pass and turned it into a 61-yard play. Holmes scored on the next play to secure the upset.

That win would be the standout moment for Mackovic at Texas. The Longhorns fell to 4–7 in 1997 and Mackovic, considered an outsider by many Texas fans, was fired at the end of the season. Texas again searched for a new coach. Little did anyone know that the new coach would raise the Texas program to a level of success not seen since the retirement of Royal in 1976.

Texas hired Mack Brown in 1998. The team went 9–3 that season.

5

A RETURN TO GLORY

TEXAS CONTINUED TO PRODUCE MORE WINNING SEASONS THAN LOSING SEASONS AFTER DARRELL ROYAL LEFT. BUT IT COULD NOT MAINTAIN THE CONSISTENT SUCCESS IT EXPERIENCED IN THE 1960S AND EARLY 1970S. THAT ALL CHANGED WHEN MACK BROWN WAS HIRED.

Brown quickly embraced the school's rich tradition. He welcomed all former Texas players to practice. He also developed a strong relationship with Royal. Brown often asked for Royal's advice and invited him to practices.

Brown's success started in his first season. The Longhorns finished 9–3 and beat Mississippi State in the Cotton Bowl. After the SWC broke apart, the game started including a Big 12 team each year. Leading the way for Texas was senior running back Ricky Williams. That season, he rushed for 2,124 yards and won the Heisman Trophy. In the regular season finale against Texas A&M, Williams ran for 259 yards to break

WATCH RICKY RUN

Not since the days of Earl Campbell had Texas fans seen a running back as talented as Ricky Williams. He was a two-time All-American and a three-time first-team All-Big 12 selection. Williams also was the first player to win the Doak Walker Award, given to the top running back in the nation each season, twice.

Williams graduated from Texas holding numerous NCAA and Texas rushing records. He finished his career with 21 NCAA records and 46 Longhorn records. Some of his NCAA records were career rushing yards (6,279), all-purpose yards (7,206), rushing touchdowns (72), total touchdowns (75), scoring (452 points), games with a touchdown (33), and 200-yard games (11).

Tony Dorsett's record and become the NCAA's all-time leading rusher. The record-breaking yards came on a 60-yard touchdown run.

While Williams was finishing his career at Texas in 1998, quarterback Major Applewhite was starting his. Applewhite set Texas freshman records in passing yards and touchdowns in 1998. He and Williams grabbed the attention of the nation when they guided the Longhorns to a 20–16 road win over the seventh-ranked Nebraska Cornhuskers. Williams rushed for 150 yards, while Applewhite threw for 269 yards and two touchdowns.

The Longhorns had another outstanding quarterback named Chris Simms. He took over the starting role as a junior in 2001. The Longhorns rolled to a 10–1 regular season record and a berth in the Big 12 Championship Game.

The third-ranked Longhorns faced number nine Colorado. Texas was favored to win. But Colorado built a 29–10 lead in the second quarter, as Simms threw three interceptions. Brown inserted Applewhite into

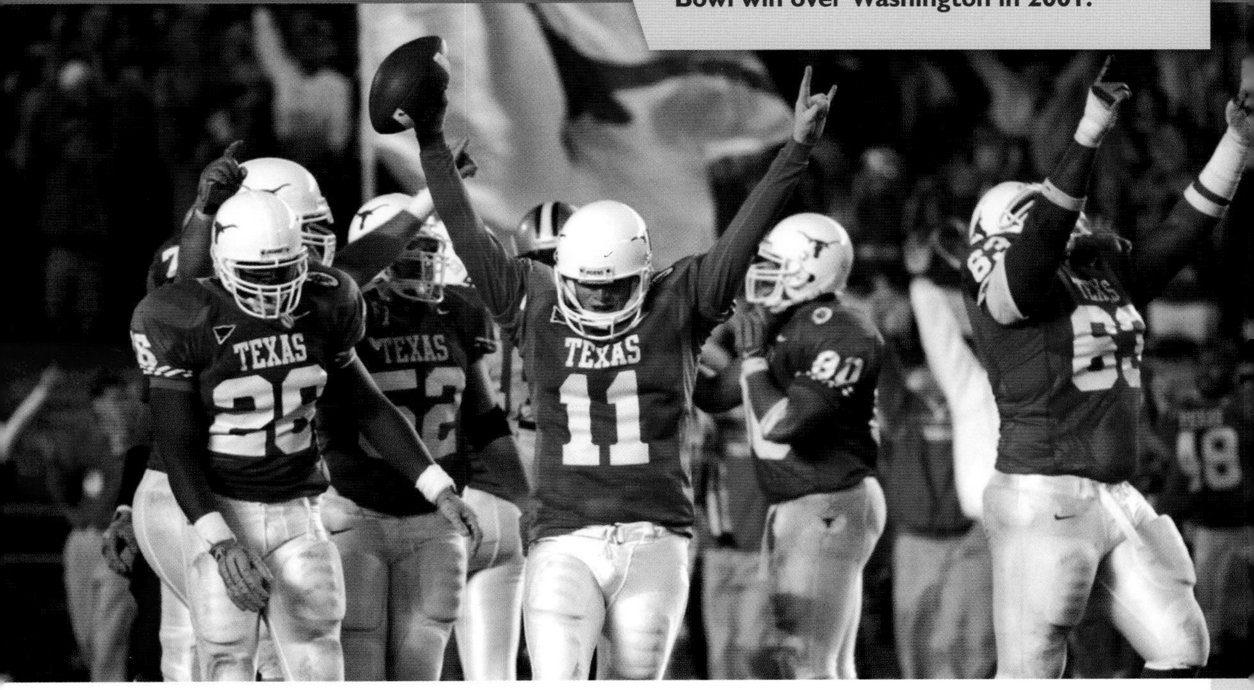

Texas quarterback Major Applewhite celebrates during the team's Holiday Bowl win over Washington in 2001.

the game, and the Longhorns immediately scored on a 79-yard pass to B. J. Johnson. But the deficit was too big to overcome. Colorado upset Texas 39–37. The loss kept the Longhorns from playing in the BCS Championship Game.

Simms and sophomore running back Cedric Benson led the way in 2002. Texas finished 11–2 and beat Louisiana State University in the Cotton Bowl. Benson rushed for 1,293 yards that year. He followed that with 1,360 rushing yards in 2003.

Junior Chance Mock started the season as the top Longhorns quarterback. But freshman Vince Young was the starter by the end of the year. He threw for 1,155 yards and rushed for 998.

DID YOU KNOW?

Cedric Benson is one of only three Texas running backs to record three consecutive 1,000-yard rushing seasons. Chris Gilbert also had three. And Ricky Williams is the only Longhorns running back to accomplish the feat four times.

Texas entered the 2004 season ranked seventh. The Longhorns' only loss was a 12–0 defeat by number two Oklahoma. It was Texas' fifth straight loss to the Sooners. Oklahoma held Young to 8-for-23 passing for 86 yards. Benson gained just 92 yards rushing on 23 carries.

Texas ended the season by beating Michigan in a thrilling Rose Bowl game. Michigan took a 37–35 lead with 3:04 remaining in the game. But Young marched the Longhorns down the field. Senior kicker Dusty Mangum kicked a wobbly 37-yard field goal as time expired to give Texas the 38–37 win. Young ran for 192 yards and four touchdowns and threw for 180 yards and one touchdown in the game.

The win gave the Longhorns a seven-game winning streak to end the season strong. Texas would extend its winning streak to 20 games by going undefeated in 2005 and beating USC 41–38 in the Rose Bowl to win the championship.

Young decided to skip his senior season and head to the NFL in 2006. With Young gone, Texas turned to freshman Colt McCoy to be the quarterback. He struggled early in the season. But he soon proved he was capable of leading the Longhorns. Texas finished the year 10–3.

Texas quarterback Colt McCoy throws a pass during Texas' 63–31 victory over Baylor in 2006.

McCoy threw for 2,570 yards and 29 touchdowns. Freshman receiver Jordan Shipley also established himself that season.

The duo had a breakout season in 2008. McCoy threw for 3,859 yards and 34 touchdowns. Shipley hauled in 89 passes for 1,060 yards and 11 touchdowns as Texas went 12–1.

The team's lone loss was to number six Texas Tech. Top-ranked Texas lost 39–33 when Texas Tech scored in the final seconds of the game. The Longhorns ended the season with a 24–21 victory over Ohio State in the Fiesta Bowl.

In 2009, only Texas Tech and Oklahoma came within 10 points of Texas during the regular season. But the Longhorns received a scare

McCOY TO SHIPLEY

From 2006–09, Colt McCoy and Jordan Shipley accounted for thousands of yards on the field. McCoy set school records with 13,253 passing yards and 112 touchdowns during his career. He left Texas with a then NCAA record 45 wins as a starter.

His favorite receiver was Shipley. He ranked first in Texas history in receptions (248) and second in yards (3,191) and touchdowns (33). As a senior, Shipley set school single-season records for receptions (116) and receiving yards (1,485), and he tied for first with 13 touchdowns.

from twenty-first ranked Nebraska in the Big 12 title game. The Cornhuskers' defense was outstanding and shut down Texas' high-powered offense. The Longhorns needed a 46-yard field goal by senior kicker Hunter Lawrence as time expired to pull out a 13–12 win and earn a berth in the BCS National Championship Game against Alabama.

The game was a matchup of Texas' offense against Alabama's defense. But McCoy, who threw for 3,521 yards and 27 touchdowns that season, was knocked out of the game in the first quarter with a shoulder injury. Freshman quarterback Garrett Gilbert took over.

Alabama built a 24–6 lead at halftime. Texas rallied in the second half. Gilbert threw touchdown passes of 44 and 28 yards to Shipley to make it 24–21 with 6:15 remaining in the game. But on the Longhorns' next possession, Gilbert lost a fumble when he was sacked. Alabama scored three plays later to take a 10-point lead. Gilbert threw an interception on Texas' next drive, and Alabama scored to win the game 37–21.

With both McCoy and Shipley gone to the NFL in 2010, the Longhorns struggled throughout the season. Gilbert was unable to

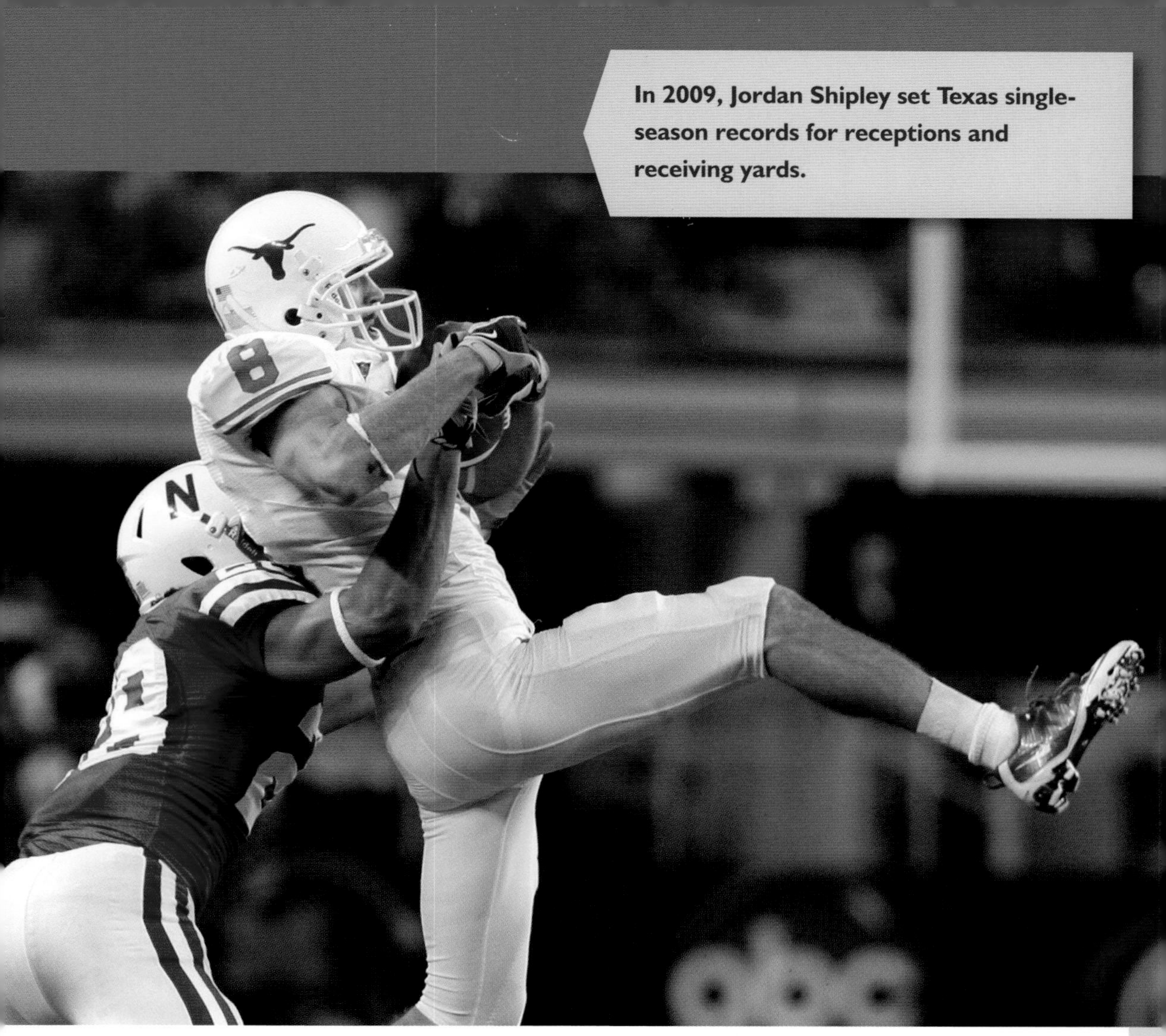

In 2009, Jordan Shipley set Texas single-season records for receptions and receiving yards.

match the magic of McCoy and Young, as Texas finished 5–7. It was the program's first losing season since 1997.

Quarterback Case McCoy and receiver Jaxson Shipley followed their older brothers to Texas. They helped form a young team that finished the 2011 regular season 7–5 and earned an invitation to the Holiday Bowl. But with Mack Brown in charge and a rich tradition to build on, fans expect Texas to be a dangerous team year after year.

TIMELINE

1893

On November 30, the University of Texas defeats Dallas Football Club 18–16 in its first ever game.

1894

Texas beats rival Texas A&M 38–0 in the first game between the two schools.

1920

The undefeated Longhorns complete their perfect season by beating the undefeated Texas A&M Aggies 7–3 on November 25.

1943

In their first bowl game, the Longhorns defeat fifth-ranked Georgia Tech 14–7 in the Cotton Bowl on January 1.

1963

Number two Texas beats number one Oklahoma 28–7 on October 12 to become the top-ranked team in the country. The win propels the Longhorns to their first national title.

1971

Ninth-ranked Notre Dame upsets number one Texas 24–11 in the Cotton Bowl on January 1 to snap the Longhorns' 30-game winning streak. Already awarded the national title by the UPI, the loss prevents Texas from claiming the AP national title.

1976

Darrell Royal coaches his final game. The Longhorns defeat Arkansas 29–12 on December 4 to send the legendary coach out with a win.

1977

Running back Earl Campbell becomes the first Texas player to win the Heisman Trophy. Campbell led the nation in rushing that season with 1,744 yards and finished his Texas career with 4,443 yards rushing.

1978

The Longhorns enter the Cotton Bowl ranked first in the country on January 1. But Notre Dame upsets Texas 38–10.

1984

Second-ranked Texas loses to number seven Georgia 10–9 in the Cotton Bowl on January 2. The loss keeps the Longhorns from winning the national title.

1964

Top-ranked Texas defeats second-ranked Navy and its Heisman Trophy-winning quarterback Roger Staubach 28–6 in the Cotton Bowl on January 1. It caps off an 11–0 season and secures Texas' first national championship.

1965

Fifth-ranked Texas faces Alabama, crowned national champion after a perfect regular season, in the Sugar Bowl on January 1. Ernie Koy rushes for 133 yards to lead Texas to a 21–17 win.

1969

Playing in the "Game of the Century" on December 6 against Arkansas, top-ranked Texas rallies from a 14–0 deficit to beat the second-ranked Razorbacks 15–14 and win the school's second national title.

1970

Top-ranked Texas upends number nine Notre Dame 21–17 on January 1 to complete a perfect 1969 season. The Longhorns trail 17–14 late in the game before Billy Dale scores on a short run for the winning touchdown.

1970

Number one Texas defeats number four Arkansas 42–7 on December 5 to win the UPI national title for the second straight season.

1995

Number nine Texas beats sixteenth ranked Texas A&M to secure the final SWC title and snap the Aggies' 31-game home winning streak on December 2.

1996

Texas upsets number three Nebraska 37–27 in the inaugural Big 12 Conference Championship Game.

1998

Running back Ricky Williams races 60 yards for a touchdown against Texas A&M to become the NCAA all-time career rushing leader on November 29. Williams wins the Heisman Trophy.

2006

Number two Texas faces defending national champion and top-ranked USC for the national title on January 4. Quarterback Vince Young scores the winning touchdown and adds the two-point conversion to give the Longhorns a 41–38 victory.

2010

After the departure of quarterback Colt McCoy and wide receiver Jordan Shipley, Texas finishes 5–7. It is the team's first losing season since 1997.

QUICK STATS

PROGRAM INFO
University of Texas Varsity (1893–1903)
University of Texas Longhorns (1904–)

NATIONAL CHAMPIONSHIPS
(* DENOTES SHARED TITLE)
1963, 1969, 1970*, 2005

OTHER ACHIEVEMENTS
BCS bowl appearances (1999–): 2
Big 12 championships (1996–): 3
Southwest Conference championships (1915–95): 26
Bowl record: 25–22–2

HEISMAN TROPHY WINNERS
Earl Campbell, 1977
Ricky Williams, 1998

KEY PLAYERS
(POSITION[S]; SEASONS WITH TEAM)
Scott Appleton (OT/DT; 1961–63)
Major Applewhite (QB; 1998–2001)
Cedric Benson (RB; 2001–04)
Earl Campbell (RB; 1974–77)
Tony Degrate (DT; 1982–84)
Peter Gardere (QB; 1989–92)
Bobby Layne (QB; 1944–47)
Colt McCoy (QB; 2006–09)
Tommy Nobis (LB/OL; 1963–65)
James Saxton (RB; 1959–61)
Jordan Shipley (WR; 2006–09)
Kenneth Sims (DT; 1978–81)
Ricky Williams (RB; 1995–98)
Vince Young (QB; 2003–05)

KEY COACHES
Dana X. Bible (1937–46):
63–31–3; 2–0-1 (bowl games)
Mack Brown (1998–):
141–39–0; 9–4 (bowl games)
Darrell Royal (1957–76):
167–47–5; 8–7-1 (bowl games)

HOME STADIUM
Darrell K Royal-
Texas Memorial Stadium (1924–)

* All statistics through 2011 season

QUOTES & ANECDOTES

The Main Building, known as the tower, stands 308 feet (93.9 m) tall in the center of the University of Texas campus. During the season, the top of the tower glows orange after each football victory. The tower is lit entirely in orange after wins against Texas A&M, or after winning a regular season or conference title. If the Longhorns win a national title in any sport, the tower is lit entirely in orange with a "#1" displayed by turning on certain lights inside the building.

Texas football coaches traditionally have ties to the program. Some played for the team during their college years and many were assistant coaches at the school. But Darrell Royal was different. He grew up in Oklahoma and later played for the rival Sooners. There he learned the game from legendary coach Bud Wilkinson. Despite his Oklahoma roots, Royal became a Texas legend thanks to winning three national titles and never suffering a losing season in 20 years as coach.

"We couldn't do much about the negativity toward us, so we focused on the accomplishment. The satisfaction far outweighed any negativity, believe me. I'm sure the bad feelings remained nationally, but we just thought about having achieved our goals, finally." —Texas offensive lineman David McWilliams on the Longhorns' win over Navy in 1963, weeks after the assassination of President John F. Kennedy in Dallas. Entering the game, many football fans around the country wanted Navy to win due to the events that occurred in Dallas.

GLOSSARY

All-American
A player chosen as one of the best amateurs in the country in a particular activity.

conference
In sports, a group of teams that plays each other each season.

deficit
The amount by which a team trails another team.

draft
A system used by professional sports leagues to select new players in order to spread incoming talent among all teams. The NFL Draft is held each spring.

dynasty
A team that maintains its position of power for a long time.

elude
To avoid somebody or something.

legend
An extremely famous person, especially in a particular field.

momentum
A continued strong performance based on recent success.

poll
A voting system in which people rank the best teams in the country.

recruit
To entice a player to come to a certain school to play on its basketball team. A player being sought after is known as a recruit.

retire
To officially end one's career. If a team retires a jersey number, no future player is allowed to wear it for that team.

rival
An opponent that brings out great emotion in a team, its fans, and its players.

rivalry
When opposing teams bring out great emotion in each team, its fans, and its players.

FOR MORE INFORMATION

FURTHER READING

Canning, Whit. *Longhorns For Life.* Champaign, IL: Sports Publishing, LLC, 2006.

Hawthorne, Bobby. *Longhorn Football: An Illustrated History.* Austin, TX: The University of Texas Press, 2007.

Wangrin, Mark. *Horns! A History: The Story of Longhorns Football.* New York: Simon & Schuster, 2006.

WEB LINKS

To learn more about the Texas Longhorns, visit ABDO Publishing Company online at **www.abdopublishing.com**. Web sites about the Longhorns are featured on our Book Links page. These links are routinely monitored and updated to provide the most current information available.

PLACES TO VISIT

College Football Hall of Fame
111 South St. Joseph St.
South Bend, IN 46601
1-800-440-FAME (3263)
www.collegefootball.org

This hall of fame and museum highlights the greatest players and moments in the history of college football.

Darrell K Royal-Texas Memorial Stadium
2100 San Jacinto Boulevard
Austin, TX 78712
512-471-3333
www.texassports.com/facilities/royal-memorial-stadium.html

This has been Texas' home field since 1924. Self-guided tours are available seven days a week.

The Mike Campbell-Bobby Moses Jr. Football Trophy Room
2100 San Jacinto Boulevard
Austin, TX 78712
402-472-2263
www.texassports.com/sports/m-footbl/spec-rel/fb-trophy-room.html

The football trophy room is a tribute to Texas' football past and present.

INDEX

ABOUT THE AUTHOR

J Chris Roselius is a freelance writer based in Houston, Texas. A graduate of the University of Texas, he has written more than a dozen books on a variety of topics. He has also won several awards for feature and column writing from the Associated Press during his career. Roselius enjoys spending his spare time with his wife and coaching his two children in Little League baseball.